Fourteen Short Essays

(1994)

*

Traumear

Titles of Essays

Justice	1
Help	2
Essay	4
You and Your Soul	5
'Leidenschaft'	8
Out of Drabness	11
Christendom	15
To Love God	19
Wisdom	24
Thinking Becomes Creation	31
Time	38
The Force Against Which Nothing Can Stand	42
The Truth	47
The Incarnate Spirit	53

*

Short Essays

1

Justice

Be just. Treat men as men, women as women and horses as horses. And let it make a difference to you whether the sun shines, whether it's morning or afternoon, and keep in mind the impression you are likely to make, on account of your age, looks, general disposition; that smoothes the path for any useful influence.

Be just to things, don't treat them like people. A pup was left tied outside the bakery after closing hours. A well-meaning lady cut it loose, whereupon it rushed into the traffic and was killed.

Be just to the occasion. Sitting next to an ogre on the bus. Writing a letter while the wind outside rages in the shrubbery. When you agree to perform a service for someone, that's one occasion; while you do it, that's another. We are on our earth because it's the best place for us. Wonderful what we can make of it!

An unjust existence is forever lived elsewhere. I stress the sense of fit. If you visit an invalid, three minutes of actually being there is worth infinitely more than half an hour while your mind strays to nonsense. I watch children. Sometimes they haven't yet been quite spoiled for the present. Unjust treatment makes them wilt. Injustice turns them into problems.

Be just to yourself. You are here for a reason. Find out what it is. Ask yourself: Why should I be standing here rather than someone else? Your own self is your nature, not people's supposed plans for you and their estimations and opinions of you.

Hope to find your own nature. Religions falsify. The thirst for justice is not quenched but expressed if you become one of

1

many – or worse, one of all. A human being is not a drop in the ocean. A person is not a pebble on the beach. All the same, no two drops, no two pebbles, are exactly alike.

What is just is appropriate. Whatever you treat justly reveals itself as wonderful. Your sense of wonder can develop once you've made a habit of justice in your approach. The sense of fit, of propriety – of wonder. Not until then will I listen to what you tell me of accurate facts and correct data. The extinct sciences are unjust. They look with impudent eyes, and usually through mechanical instruments. The more sophisticated instrument forces from things a renewed cry for justice. This cry is taken for a sign of progress. Then the torture recommences. What nature confesses under torture is no self-revelation but the shame and guilt of the torturer.

Not until I let you be yourself can I be truly myself; then we can communicate. If your nature has been perverted I shall treat you as if it had not. Be just to a degenerate soul by treating it as if it were precious, as a soul. Or not as if it were, but because it is.

*

2

Help

On the connection – in my own mind at the moment, if in no way otherwise – between help and half: help someone, be a half, for his sake, so that he may be the other half.

We need help when we're not whole – not hale, not holy. But being half, that's not being unwhole. It's like being whole, but for a reason.

'I'm only half alive' you say, and sadly, with right. An 'only half' is not a half. Mere appearances are not appearances. You 'only live' when you don't really live. So go ahead and halve yourself, and then I can become the other half, because at the moment I'm only half alive.

It's a quaint notion. Not like that simpering sympathy, when I pretend to be ill to make you who are ill feel better. Surely that's misguided. Whether sympathy is necessarily a pretence, that's another question. But look at it this way: When you're not well, how does it make you feel if the fellow next to you flaunts his health? When you're miserable and I say to you: 'I'm ever so happy! How can you be miserable!' – how does that affect you? Would you rather I pretended to be miserable along with you? Myself, I would expect that you can afford to do without both.

Be wretched with the wretched: Does that mean 'pretend to be wretched' or rather 'be really wretched along with me'? Perhaps it means neither. Perhaps your malaise has a certain form and I, for the time being and for your sake, can adopt that form? Or perhaps I can adopt the obverse of that form, since the form of a reality has a face and an obverse?

First I would have to accept that you are really unwell. And then I would have to believe that you can be helped. Can I really accept the former if I don't believe the latter?

Our human heart is mercifully inclined. It makes little of itself so that its friend and companion may grow bigger. It halves itself. It divides itself into pieces and gives itself away, aware of its substantial infinitude. Has god not helped us by dividing himself and becoming little for our sake as the meek and mild and suffering Jesus? What a let-down for my triumphant ego! Right at this moment, cognizant of our need, he divides himself up into particles to feed us. Always there are basketfuls left over.

He halves himself to help us, can we afford to do otherwise for one another?

A brilliant mathematical supposition – the half is to the whole as the Messiah is to god. "Love god and follow me." Make room in yourselves for one another. Don't pretend. Don't really get sick along with me either. I need you whole. But not

3

blatantly, boastfully, callously whole. I need you as a whole half, if you take my meaning.

Or perhaps you can make of yourself one and a half, then I can fit my mere half in and we can become two?

The ethic of fraction. They pierced him, but not a bone of him was broken. Not a mere half, if you want to help, but a true half – on my behalf.

*

3

Essay

What it brings us – there we have the secret of the essay. That our human spirit leaps into the unknown with the firm conviction, hopefully based on common faith, that it can only learn good things and nothing to our detriment. I challenge anyone to come up with a more exciting adventure – and yet it's a silly challenge; I would have to pity the one who took it up.

The leap into the unknown for the sake of knowledge – in other words, nothing derived, nothing calculated or dreamt – and above all, nothing invented. How so not? Because everything in that realm of the unknown has to come to us as a gift. We leave reality entirely to its own devices and only place ourselves in such a way that, if it chose, it might inform us.

But as you would expect, it always chooses. To my immense satisfaction I have learnt that. What I call reality has it in for me as a human being and I honour what it has in for me. I think that is why it trusts me, because I honour it. The search for knowledge, for me, is worship in reality and I confess that none of my friends try to argue me out of this. They seem to respect my freedom and in my own quiet mind I thank them for this respect.

The serious essay as a literary form specializes in this leap of faith for new knowledge. In other words it would teach us and show us this leap, give us courage by example for taking it. The subject- or object-matter is irrelevant to this main thrust. Call it the pretext. The real purpose of an essay is to prove to us that the fear of the unknown can be overcome and to ingrain in us the habit – the good ritual, if you like – of doing it. On the negative side, it should suffice for us that we sense the lowest seam on the gown of this fear and already we leap beyond it. On the positive side we believe we don't have to wait for the fear before we exercise our spirit of adventure on the green field of truth.

What is it that makes us most reluctant to set out? Self-complacency. When we're perfectly happy, why should we try to come out of ourselves? The answer to this is simple: When you're perfectly happy, that's when you should try to come out of yourself. If you don't, you run the risk of stagnation, of corruption. Perfect happiness has to be put to good use or it traps us. The ensuing affliction may be spiritual, moral or physical.

The essay as a discipline applies itself to this onset of desuetude. An essay makes us more alert to our human nature as a generator rather than as a lazy way to be. Get off your behind, it says, and walk into the promised land. Invest, don't malinger.

So don't expect to be flattered, to be told pleasantries. The unprovocative essay is not worth its salt. It must touch on your hoard of prejudice, on your fortress of superstition, on your system of hypocrisy. Otherwise how can the leap into the unknown ever become desirable for you? Ignorance would define us.

*

4

You and Your Soul

Do you have a soul or are you a soul? Presumably what we are cannot be what we have.

5

But who wants to know about souls nowadays. Either we have lost them or they have never really existed.

What does it mean when god requires our soul? Some would say it means that we die. We step up to god one day and say: Please give us a soul so that we may live. But my goodness me, says god, how could you be speaking to me if you did not live? No, have another think about it. You are not yet on the right track. If I told you the long and short of it, in so many words, you would never grow up. My wish is to be surrounded by responsible men and spontaneous women.

Very well, then, so each one of us presumably is a soul. We are human beings, so we are souls. But then we cannot 'have' a soul – or 'lose' it, for that matter. Or the creator has made us as souls, and if we exist because we are sparks from him who is the great fire, then these sparks cannot be extinguished. After all, the great fire cannot go out.

So our own reason convicts us of an error in thinking here. Because we have known of persons who have died. They disappeared from before our eyes while we spoke to them and were transformed into animal existences. It suddenly became impossible to communicate with them. They used the same words but spoke a different language. I know a young man who changes back and forth like this three or four times during the course of two hours. No, after his glass of vodka he is liable to flip in and out of the soul four times in four minutes – it makes my head spin. I have shouted at him – to no avail. One minute he allows for me, responds to me, the next minute something takes over from where he has left off. Where there was a soul there is none.

I would be happy with a soul that rests in me as a function of my being. As I am, so my soul. If I am not, no soul. If I am human, my soul is human. This opens up a variety of possibilities. My soul would be an indicator of my being. If I were divine, I would have a divine soul, and I would know that I was divine by way of knowing my divine soul. In other words, thanks to my soul I know myself – meaning that I know how I am, what state I'm in, what I'm in need of, what the next step for me is, and so on.

However, not only is my soul the criterion of my being, of who I am, how I am and what I am – and specifically of the fact that I am – but, in important addition to this, my soul is functional. It operates. How I am and who I am etc., makes an impression on you, on others and on my environment. Only while I am does my soul operate, and it operates as I am. I can be as I wish, I can be happy, glad, joyful, unafraid, etc. – my soul is an indication of this to me and a communication of it to you and others.

Consequently by tending to my soul I inadvertently tend to you and to others. Is this not the secret of true love? Never mind that now. Enough said that my soul as functional and operational is equally and at the same time my soul as harmonious and constant.

So why bother with a soul at all? Why not confine ourselves to being and doing? What I am and what I do – or better, who I am and what I do – are evidently of one piece. In that case, as long as we never neglect to teach our soul as both being and doing, we might do well to make use of such an expression as soul again, to emphasize that 'one piece', that crucial point of articulation from which we both are and do. When joyless arthritis sets in, we become judgmental and ineffective; or, if the connection is lost altogether, we become monsters of impersonal inversion of dogmatic careerism. Not a pretty prospect!

In any case, we would do better to get rid of that concept of a soul in a body now for all time. It sounds too much like baked beans in a tin. Let the problematic psyche animate the supposedly unregenerate flesh, then we know where to go and what to avoid. Keeping body and soul together, that's a dodo. Keep the psyche and the flesh together if you must, but you have my permission to make your soul your priority, your being and doing, all of a piece, and as body or mind, as body <u>and</u> mind, physically – concrete. Examine yourself: Are you a solid, active soul or a psyche flapping in the wind?

*

5

'Leidenschaft'

Via a comment by Lichtenberg on Sterne I providentially arrive at the German word 'Leidenschaft', translated in the dictionary as passion. 'Leiden' means to suffer. 'Schaft' has to do with 'schaffen', to do, to make, to work, to create. Compare the English suffix '-ment'.

What sort of a work do we achieve through suffering? Let's light the fuse under that question. Let's get a few things straight. When we suffer we're not in pain. That's our reason for suffering. To avoid pain? Not quite. We suffer so as to remove the hindrance we have caused to good change.

Ah, it still sounds as if we could suffer accidentally. But not a single human act is less unintentional. Bang goes the neat discrepancy between action and passion. To suffer means to act? I should have thought it meant just the opposite: to put up with, to have to put up with, to find yourself as having to undergo, that sort of thing.

It means what we want it to mean. Every word means what we want it to mean. It all depends on who we are. A scoundrel turns words into labels between breakfast and lunch. Then his children assume that words are labels and this renders them speechless. So they suppose they have nothing to say. Their human nature is undone because they lack the tools for saying it. Language has become dysfunctional. Then we do violence to labels to get back to the sense of things. Who is willing to manage the household of language? Certainly not the linguist. But the common man is willing. He has something to say and

8

he refuses to be content with half-measures. They will hang labels around his neck and chase him into the wilderness but that's where he needs to be in any case, to practice his speech. Let him marvel at the effect of true speech in the wilderness. He tries a few traditional labels and the thorns press in, the beasts move closer. Then he speaks his first word, lo and behold, justice! Something becomes itself. For days he has smashed his way through the undergrowth but he only has ended up bleeding and in the soup, and with yet another label around his neck: mixer of metaphors! Right, he says, enough of this crap, I am going to suffer. Let them do their worst, I shall open my heart to them. They probably don't know what they're doing. – And the thorns recede, the beasts look respectful, a glass of water appears in his hand (or on a sandy patch beside his elbow).

Has he not done something? He ignored the sweat on his brow and the fear in the pit of his stomach and he opened his heart – and he stopped resisting the evil all around him. He forgave the wilderness.

He has gained an advantage. Will he press it? Or does he congratulate himself on his indolence? How can he press his advantage? The beasts and the thorns respectfully hold back for the moment, waiting for his next move. They have no problem with accepting that he has made a meaningful move. It came over them without their notice. The effect on them was immediate. But now they hang on his lips. Is he going to speak? Will he say something? Or will he smile apologetically, make a routine gesture and crawl into his own pathetic feelings?

He has arrived on the threshold of the second half of the word Leidenschaft: – schaft, from schaffen: to make, to create. Is his passion going to be a halfway thing? Will he stop halfway up the stairs and get cold feet?

He does not. He insists that his heart remain open and his soul vibrant. He is occupied with himself like never before.

The very elements clamour for attention. An infinity of time passes. Still he suffers the apparent need to struggle against the lack of expression. He suffers in silence. The silence is crucial. It's as if he were waiting to make contact with the truth in his own loins. Consciousness alone occurs to him as folly. Though he sees no path, he will not be side-tracked. Passion at its best. "My God, why have you forsaken me!" In the absence of everything and in the presence of nothing he continues to suffer, even though there is no more pain as such; he persists with an open heart, an alert mind, a patient body. There are those who would tell him to catch himself on and strike out while the enemy is down but he sees it otherwise. He cannot any more see an enemy. He persists though he has nothing to persist against except a lack of persistence. Again there are those who say that this is not possible. But why should he argue, when he is doing it? Indeed the essence of his perseverance is that he refuses to pretend that something exists when in fact it does not. If nothing exists, for him, then so be it, he can take it. The normal passage of time leaves him cold. He has the tail of eternity, of immortality, in his hand and he won't let go. Not for man nor beast nor the weeping of women will he let go.

He has come to the conclusion meanwhile that while he does what he does, something is happening for him. He cannot quite give it a name yet, but perhaps soon he will, unless of course he decides that it desires to remain nameless. The secret source of language is not to be outspoken, though now and again we have to revive an old expression or press a new combination of sounds into service.

He knows in himself now the fruits of his suffering and he will never again strive for some supernatural alleviation of his state in the wilderness. The wilderness is there for a purpose and while his suffering does its work, that purpose is seen to, is matched, and the hindrance in himself, for which he had decided to take the responsibility – has subsided. The wilderness was nothing but the outward sign of his own inward immaturity.

Was it wisdom that accumulated, while he suffered? Was wisdom the effect of his passion, his 'Leidenschaft', the outcome of his undergoing? Perhaps it was, this time. Next time it may be something else. A human universe in the making. A perpetual alliance of his brother and himself. Or finally a union in the flesh that lasts, in spite of afflictions and indiscretions.

*

6

Out of Drabness

A thoroughly drab day – not rationally, when you recollect the stages, but at the moment, in depth, definitely drab. But having said that, things begin to pick up. A little light glimmers.

Have you no imagination? Get onto the back of a horse and canter down that forest path. Wood pigeons break out of the pines, rattle across the field. You are one person and at the same time another. You do and you observe yourself doing. But your observation is really, as it says, a service. You begin to enjoy your own company – which means nothing more complicated than that you have begun to be yourself and that you enjoy it.

Of course being yourself means doing something. Even if you were only to breathe, intentionally, that would be doing something. There are those who have made a science out of breathing. And why not? Is it less important, less philanthropic, to breathe meaningfully than to take the responsibility, as a banker, for the nation's cash? How you do it, and in whose name, that matters more sometimes than what you do. In any case, you cannot be yourself unless you do something you respect, and only then can you enjoy living.

The fog closes in. The path has become marshy. Gusts of wind whip the mane of your horse left and right. There, a light in the trees. A charcoal burner's hut. Thank goodness! Trite perhaps, but a relief all the same. Now hope flashes across the sky. The mind opens. Time is no longer problematic. What did you call it? A drab day? You yourself were drab. You should have looked around you right away. But I know, you didn't have the eyes. Was it after a heavy meal that you finally turned to me? Pardon me, I take that back, I had no intention of bringing myself into the picture; it happened, accidentally. But accidents do happen and then we do well to make the best of them.

Very well, now that I've come out of hiding we can have a conversation. How are you disposed? Are you in a good mood? Are you glad to see me?

"I have reservations. You complicate matters when I was not aware of their existence. Now you smile, and I wonder what to make of that."

Ah, you feel inferior to me. That's unavoidable – but unjust. I am nothing more than a duplication of yourself. However I am nothing less either. Self-duplication was once, by a philosopher, called the heartbeat of creativity. Who else now would have told you that? Who would have had the courage?

"What I ask myself is, why did you not assume the personality of that charcoal burner? You might have adopted a filthy daughter with a golden heart and a charming face under the soot. Would that not have turned out much more ... more ..."

Are you stuck?

"Instead you turn into a voice from outer space."

Did you not set out to write an essay?

"That's correct."

And do you suppose I was out of the country when you made that decision?

"That's a real head-scratcher of a question."

Not only do I know what you decide but also what you feel. Just now you felt incompetent because nothing occurred to you to ask me. You wanted to take intelligent advantage of me but you couldn't think how. You imagined yourself side by side with me as we are at the moment and you asked yourself: How can I most usefully proceed? There must be a way forward that has not yet been tried by me. But your horizon, or ours, actually, appeared disappointingly narrow – although not drab. You wished yourself endowed with more power, more capacity for action, but you desired to remain in my company at the same time. Now what about this: Can you tell me what goes on in my own head?

"You are not what I would call a critical person, but you delight in the minutest of observations. At this moment your head is full of fancy notions with respect to the future, and I confess, that worries me. You speak like someone who is not entirely in touch with his own humanity. As I say this, you blush. It reminds you of fears you have harboured, doubts you have not quite been able to ascertain. At this very moment I discern in you a process of self-mortification. Maybe you overextended yourself – ethically? Be glad I came along on my essay, on my horse. I lured you out of your self-complacency. You were tempted to show me the ropes, but by giving in to that temptation you also made personal contact with me. Allow me to place the emphasis on that. I can see it's a sore point. I would say that you are much more accustomed to educating individuals than to union with another heart."

Please, go ahead. I don't trust myself to speak just now.

"The union of two hearts – what a lot of head-work is required to achieve that! What a great deal of listening to others, not only quietly but in actual silence! And most of all, what about the ability to notice another man's weakness and to consciously become weak with him, so that you might come up with appropriate strength? Could you walk with me a distance

13

so as to mend your ways, which were not your ways before you accompanied me? Do I speak in riddles?"

You do. But I asked for it. I shall puzzle it out at leisure.

"What's wrong?"

I feel tired. Lethargic. I droop like a rose at the end of summer. How long to the end of your essay?

"A bit more than a page."

Will you support me if I falter?

"We are in this together. By betraying you I would betray myself. If I give you up to the forces of dissolution, I saddle myself with untold problems."

But be specific. How can we be of service to each other, now that the creative energy has waned?

"You ignore the passion of life. Energy in itself is nothing, nothing but a sensation. I suggest we become friends. Here, I extend the hand of friendship. I commit myself to a higher form of life. A worthwhile essay. What do you say?"

What are the implications for the future?

"That we bear each other's afflictions. That we search each other out in oblivion. That we work towards a common humanity. That we lose track of each other at our own peril."

I can see nothing but good in that. I accept your hand in friendship. I also feel a little stupid.

"How is that?"

Friendship is such a closed book to me. The way you talk about it, is it a life's wakefulness, and a life's attentiveness?

"And a constant knowledge of gain. Two can overcome for each other with ease what would needlessly trouble the one separately. You might say that we have agreed to care more about each other than about ourselves. Now let's take it easy. I intend to lead this horse back to the stable. You may ride if you prefer. You look worn out. Stay at my lodgings overnight. Here, lean on my shoulder."

This was well worth it. A masterful accomplishment, although I feel spent. Let's look for the reward in the future.

"The immediate future."

*

7

Christendom

Christendom – say that with the eyes closed. Now say it with the eyes open. It makes a tremendous difference. Imagined on a full stomach, Christendom is a concept for a conjurer. Who is Christ? What was his first name? His Christian name was Jesus. Now several million people call themselves Christians. Some do it still and some do it again. The two lots have very little in common; they frequent separate conventicles. True, there are born-again human beings, one has met one or two. They are not born-again Christians. They frequent no conventicles at all. Christendom holds for them next to no fascination. They feel equally at home anywhere on the globe. They carry their homes with them, like snails their houses, but within.

Christendom holds hands with geography. Official declarations decide its issues. Nations and states will make or mar it. Ireland pertains to Christendom, Paddy Foyle does not. At night he sleeps just as well under the stars, does Paddy, as under that questionable roof of a collective concept. And yet if Paddy woke up to the wail of a Muezzin, how bitter his porridge would taste! And then he would get used to it. Because Paddy believes what the newspapers publish and his doctrine is dogmatic. The prevalent opinion stuffs his mattress, cleans his windows and soles his shoes. If his daughter comes home late, he chides her, or keeps quiet, or chides himself, on account of such elements as hormones, genes and temperament, not on the

15

basis of benefits gleaned from a book. Over the ages Paddy has had his knuckles rapped by the hierarchy, his cheek tweaked by the priest and who can say but that he enjoyed the attention. Out of Paddy grow forth branches past religions, beliefs and creeds; he will not be mastered by them. His master rests, maybe sleeps, in his nature. If you want to change Paddy, I suggest you examine your heart. Read Lampedusa on Paddy the Sicilian.

But where would we be without self-discipline and then without civilization! Never blame Christendom for its thoroughgoing concentration on total order, for its categorization of the classes and masses. It is that order, so it was. If ever anything replaces Christendom – but how misapplied that sounds! It's the picture that changes, the frame stays the same. One day people will not any more know what that meant: Christendom – but Jesus may live in their hearts.

The kingdom of heaven on earth: Christendom – one assumes that was the aim, the ambition – the presumption? You hang a label on yourself and then you travel abroad and beat others into submission – after you affix the opposite label to them. They don't know what you want. But eventually they give in, for the sake of a quiet life. I dare say at times the change was as good as a rest. But world conquest is not self-conquest. The Messiah whose being is not exhausted by concerns of time, space and causality is glad enough to discipline our recalcitrant selves for us and makes a better job of it than we could in a month of Sundays. All we must do is make room for him here and now. Make room and time for him, and give him cause. Then the world will tempt or threaten us no longer but we will regard it. No longer will we look for the most powerful organisation to join because power will have become the very air we breathe.

The national status of a man limits him to the consumption of a few ideals. The European is a mild-mannered vindicator, but also a helpless indicator, of race relations on the rocks. On one hand he hearkens back to Christendom. It's a mixed nostalgia, only made possible, one fears, by the prolonged shock and anaesthesia of two world wars. Ask not only what decisions are being made but, perhaps more interesting, who are the people who come forward to make themselves responsible for those decisions. From what cloth are they cut? A rocket is a charismatic shell. A sense of honour buried under red tape becomes a damp squib. Totally characterless individuals eventually parade their utter lack of individuality in front of the hall mirror where Europe stands reflected, with its lid open, on a three-legged French-polished side-table, unidentifiable trivia spilling out onto the lace-trimmed doily, in German called 'Zierdeckchen'; in French perhaps 'garde-nappe'. What were we talking about? Oh yes, the typhoon, the moon. And too much loquacity etc. etc.

And then there is the 'good' European. He has only been around for a couple of centuries but Christendom is not his favourite word today. To be good means to tolerate, to scuttle the narrow border for the wider one. Should the good European not protect his market against the good Asian, the good African, American, Australian?

It's a question of home economics, and of whether or not we make a difference between primary and secondary importance. There is truth and there is right. Where truth makes its own sense, right is not the same as where it's another label for the same thing. Once a human being has acquired a taste for personal truth and justness, he gets confused by such a thing as Christendom, as Islam, as born-again Israel. Is he looking at a sphinx? The thing is neither fish nor fowl. Professor Midlothian knows exactly what it means and he would like to explain it to him. But this particular (born-again) human being cannot cope with exact knowledge. You might as well ask him to live in a tombstone. Repeatedly he shakes his head, no, no, he can't make out the professor's meaning at all, at all. You see, a cut

17

has been made, so that now, for him, there is an outward and an inward, and when something is correct it's not necessarily true, although that doesn't mean it's false either, which confuses the professor in turn, because what he professes bleeds when you put a knife in it and after a number of years it dies. His reality is professed. If you like, he will profess good Europeanism without batting an eyelid and we are not to hinder him. Before lunch, or even earlier this morning, he might have declared himself for Christendom, though at the time he was a Christian, right in head and heart. "As long as you understand," he says. He himself is a rational animal, possibly born-again.

It's a fine thing to make contact with the earth and with all its natural boundaries, such as oceans, rivers and mountain ranges, and then to imagine that one day perhaps the only external border we will need will be acceptable by us as ready made terrestrially. The new earth is as right as the new heaven is true, and the union of the two will be our actual dwelling place. Those who live here now can vouch for the goodness of it. They incorporate in themselves the union of the two; in themselves – as a community, and as communities, never merely as individuals. One gets the impression that Christendom was invented as a basket for individuals: individual people, individual groups, institutions and states. Think what this means: We have to try to get along because we are both Christians. With those Mohammedans we don't have to try. "Yes you do, you have to try with them too," says the good European. Paddy can't make sense of this. Why should he try? He has no quarrel with them in the first place. And if he does, it won't be because they're Mohammedans or in spite of their being Christians. And your born-again human being will set the professor on one knee and the born-again Christian on his other knee so that they have to face each other and then he will talk to them like a Dutch uncle and forgive them both for all that

18

traditional and revellational (sic) nonsense. (A find: born-again Christian enthusiasm = revellation)

A man, a woman – a child: These are able to come out of themselves at a moment's notice if the chap beside them has a runny nose and needs it wiped, if his grief slops over the edge of the cup and somebody else is needed to take a sip, or if he's bursting with joy and can't possibly celebrate by himself. The melody that rises from the heart to the throat becomes a lark and a star not familiar to the astronomer and the ornithologist. In broad daylight nothing is rejected but everything is acceptable in the true light of day. The endless world, the perfect universe – the beautiful cosmos: available now, in the future, in the past, take your pick. If this were not so, would anyone in complete earnestness and sobriety sit down and write that it is so?

Prophets come and go but the word abides forever. And this is the word, that the god who makes us is allowed by us to live in us and to express himself as ourselves. Who we are, this is god's word. God cannot contradict himself. If you and I do not see eye to eye, then I have a golden opportunity to move heartily into my god by taking upon myself this misunderstanding. As for you and what you do, that need not be my business.

Our manhood, our womanhood and our childhood – our Christhood, respectively, is at stake. We can make ourselves tiny, but the moon will find us out. Our ribs are counted and should our hairs stand straight on our heads. Becoming gestures fill the air, sorrow and joy are not what they used to be – but may be better, greater: and final. Think what this means: Finally our god has arrived.

*

8

To Love God

Anyone can do it. The question is: Why bother? Why love anyone or anything? We unite ourselves with what we love,

19

become one with it. Would we not rather stand out alone? Surely the idea is to be something in our own right, such as an engineer, a wife or a pop star. I want to be an actress, she said. So she loved acting. Or did she love herself in the guise of an actress?

True love and false love. We want to become one with something, someone, other than ourselves or we want to become one with our self. This latter proposition is not so far-fetched. You insist on your self, you argue for its rights. You justify your self. This is love too, but love in reverse, and therefore destructive.

Love your neighbour as yourself: There are so many ways to mean that. You are to do this intentionally, that's interesting in the first place. Then you are to pretend that your neighbour, the person presently next to you, is you. Or perhaps you are not to pretend, but simply to make the substitution. Use that tree as firewood. Take tomorrow as a holiday. Don't pretend to use it, to take it. Do it actually and in fact. Then love your neighbour as yourself. That person standing beside you there, that's you in terms of the love you come up with. Try that out now on a few people. Give yourself a couple of weeks' practice. Then return to the previous paragraph.

At the very root of the act of love something can go wrong. It's as if we could make a bad start and then nothing but rubbish follows. When we allow the well to get dirty, the water in the dipper is dirty too.

The self – my self – when that exists, false love is even then afoot, and any loving I presume to do from then on cannot prosper, cannot be real and effective in any useful sense, because I am bound to unite myself with my self. Before I can truly love, then, I have to hate my self. As love unites me with what or whom I love, so does hate separate me from those. And I would be separate from my self. I want nothing to do with it. I want to love you, or god, but my self gets in the way and automatically

20

bends this love towards itself, excluding god, or you. My magic self. My electro-magnetic self. How the physicists study its perennial shadow out there!

*

How to hate. How to shun, to exclude, to annihilate. And then to do that to one's self. You are the one who does the hating, remember, so you cannot hate yourself; but you can hate your self. You can do it because you know that you want to love and you understand that you cannot love while this self of yours – this self-regard, this self-respect, this self-confidence – is still around.

Self-hate is the viable solution, the logical conclusion. Practice self-hate now. Keep in mind what your reason for doing it is, otherwise you will accidentally hate yourself. Or you may try, and then you throw yourself into all kinds of morbid poses, to convince yourself and to convince your self – which self, by the way, you may well have come into the way of calling your God now. That's a terrible mix-up. Your self just loves to set itself up as your God. It likes to lord it over you so that it would not occur to you ever to hate it in that healthy, joyful, inwardly detaching way. Once you have made this pact with your self that 'It shall be your God!' you become a thorough nuisance to those around you who don't at all hate themselves and who don't have such a God. They may not know now to cope with you and so they will just distance themselves from you. However, it's very likely that you will confirm their own suspicions regarding their self as a possible god and so, before you can shake a stick at your self, they have formed around you a little conclave with you as their leader. Or not with you, to be fair, but with your self as their leader, because you yourself are after all being led by your self, are you not? By now you have actually chosen to be led by your self, and that conclave around you grows. You call it humility, when you defend yourself and say: 'Not me, but my God!' meaning, of course, your self.

21

And no one else will tell you that you're wrong. No one has the right to tell you. You have the perfect right to call your self your God and worship it. Or let's put it this way: Who has the right to tell you otherwise? Are you not self-justified? Does your God not justify you? Well, you'll find that others are much more likely to stand back in awe, to either worship at your shrine along with you or else leave you to it. It's just too formidable a task to take on anyone's self. One would actually have to hate it as one's own self.

When I love you as myself, I do in fact do that, it's part of it: I hate your self as my self. And believe me we don't have to go searching for one another's self. It leaps out the first chance it gets, across the divide between me and you. My self leaps across and adds itself on to your self like an electric charge. Then you are saddled with it. For the moment I disport myself, as unsaddled. I've shaken off the burden of my self and you inadvertently have ended up with it. Something most unusual goes on now. I begin to fly and you begin to creep. I take to the air and you take to the ground. You begin to resent me for my levity, don't you. What right have I to be a blithe spirit when you feel filled up with resentment! This resentment is suddenly upon you, like an electric charge. (Actually it's the electric charge which is like your resentment, but we won't go into that now.) And myself, I walk heedlessly overtop of you, over you and your resentment. When I notice it, I become indignant, contemptuous. What right have you to spoil my fun? I'm on top of the world and you're trying to drag me down. Shame on you! You are envious of my happiness! Even now I can sense the disillusionment set into myself and I know who is to blame! Here I've burdened you with my load and instead of celebrating my liberty with me you act as though you were bearing twice the load. Ah well, there's no justice.

I try that often enough, dumping my load on others, and after a while, when nobody at all helps me celebrate my liberty, I be-

22

come disillusioned, cynical. The world is full of selfish people. I have what it takes to be happy, I've learned the knack of shrugging my shoulders, but those others, look at them, they're jealous. They evidently want me to be miserable like themselves.

I may even cultivate the art of looking burdened. If nobody wants to celebrate with me, the least I can do is celebrate by myself, behind the protection of a long face.

*

If you were in my shoes, what would you do? Don't tell me, I know. You would not only continue to hate your own self, which you did quite successfully before I came along, but in addition to this you would now also hate *my* self. You would realize how mixed up I was and, because you have a good habit of loving the person next to you, you would overcome in yourself your first impulse to kick my head in and, after having managed this lovingly, you would then continue to hate your augmented self and to love me. What a surprise that would be for me! What a shock! I'd suddenly be treading air. I would come down to the ground like a hot air balloon that has been punctured but did not burst. You would continue to love me over a period of time, while you hated your self as augmented by that extra charge of my transferred self, and my head would be in a spin. I wouldn't be able to enjoy my selfish liberty at all, not because you've resented it and envied it for me, which you didn't, but because you set me an example of freedom, and that's catching. You demonstrate to me the freedom of loving me in spite of my selfishness and I must say, that takes my self-celebrating breath away. Here I'm suddenly breathing the fresh air, the real air, of freedom! True enough, I feel a little foolish too, but you don't seem to want to abuse me for that. You seem to have my real interests at heart. I sense that, though I dare say I'm a long way from understanding it.

Shall I tell you what occurs to me? That you've shown me friendship.

And what have you done? Have you done anything much different from what you would have done – from what you would have wanted to do – if I hadn't turned up? You loved the person next to you and you hated your self. The fact that your self suddenly loomed so large that you wanted to give me a good dressing down, to wipe that smile off my face, to stuff that illegitimate happiness down my throat, that only occurred to you as a greater opportunity for love.

I don't know what to say, I'm overcome. Love is evidently bigger than I am, and there's my self that would tell me otherwise. I try to make an issue out of it but that doesn't work. My self has disappeared now, until next time, so I'm left here with the desire to learn how to do what you've just done. You loved me in spite of my self and it sobered me up. Also it left me with a distinct distaste for my self and I shouldn't wonder but that this will stand me in good stead the next time – when my self appears on the scene and promises me isolated grandeur, or the happiness of weightless flight, of careless self-sufficiency.

I can't make out where to go from here. The proper thing to do is not what I want to do, and what I feel like doing doesn't work. Love has me trapped. I am not my own master any more. I am not anyone's master. I intend to hold out here while I can. Since I know what's going on, what right have I not to be cheerful? I'm glad I'm trapped by love. Although I have nothing to hate at the moment, I can still endure.

*

9

Wisdom

Wisdom. Be wise. Not enough to be – as if that weren't tricky enough, surrounded as we are by slippery forces and undermining energies! Now we are to be wise! And is that supposed to be a skill of some sort? Can I learn how to be wise, considering what a fool I am? Who can tell me? How am I going to find out? Even if a teacher lived on my street, I wouldn't know what questions to ask him. But let me try all the same.

Teacher: First of all, the way you come here is wrong from the start. You're far too cocky. Then, you expect to be given what I have, don't you? That's wrong too. Nobody can give you wisdom or make you wise. You've either got it or you don't.

Me: Then why bother with teachers?

T: Good question. You may have it, but not know that you have it. Or, you may have the wrong way of it. Many a man travelled miles for happiness and then found it inside his own skin.

Me: So are you telling me to go home?

T: Yes. Go home. Find your home.

Me: Anything else?

T: That's entirely up to you. I didn't ask you to come here.

Me: Alright. I'm determined to find out if I'm wise. And if I am, I'm going to be wise, at least for a while, to find out what it's like and to see what I brings me in.

T: Smart fellow. Always one eye on the profit. Only a twit would do anything for nothing.

Me: So I'm smart. I wonder, is that a step towards wisdom?

T: No, but the fact that you wonder, that is. If you're smart, that only means that you know how to get to your goal. It doesn't mean that you'll choose a worthwhile goal.

Me: Wonder? But I only said that. I meant nothing by it.

T: Nonetheless you said it. Take my word for it, it's indicative. If you know how to wonder, then you're able to find out things. You're trying to find out if you're wise. What you say unconsciously is indicative. So wonder if you're wise.

Me: Very well. I'll do that. I wonder if I'm wise.

T: Aha! That's a good sign too! You were ready to take my word for something. That means you know how to trust. I saw you thinking, so you didn't agree stupidly. Smart – wonder – trust. You are really getting somewhere. Of course it still doesn't mean much. You may only find out that you're not wise.

M: I can't follow you there, I'm afraid. I distinctly felt myself straying over a borderline there. I may be wrong, but I had the impression that there was more to my last insight than pertains to the trip towards wisdom. Something new happened to me.

T: Describe it.

M: A little fearful. A spot of awe. A bit of pain, as though you had short-changed me. Also the desire to reflect and immediate reflection setting in. Add to that an inner certainty without necessarily knowing of what. A deepening experience. An increase of seriousness. Some steadiness of purpose, as in the case of growing character.

T: Easy does it.

M: I'm not straining.

T: Now tell me this. If a man rushes through the marketplace with a burning candle at noon crying: "God is dead! You have killed God!" – what happens next?

M: His candle goes out.

T: But if god is really dead, would he have needed a candle?

M: My guess would be that god is alive and the man is mad.

T: Assume he was telling the truth.

M: His candle would still go out. He was rushing.

T: Forget about the bloody candle. Assume he carried a lantern.

M: At Noon?

T: It was very cloudy.

Me: My guess is he wants to make contact symbolically – with those people. His heart goes out to them. So he accuses

26

them of a crime. Which makes him a bad man on top of being a madman. I think we should …

T: Wait. Symbolic contact, you said. For what?

M: For your and my sake. Evidently you heard about it. The momentum of a symbol is sometimes underrated. Even if he was bad and mad, that too was for our sake, and for those we speak to and live with once we go our own way.

T: Is he to get the credit?

M: He can have it from me if he wants.

T: Be serious.

M: I am. I mean it. If he were standing in front of me now and wanted me to thank him for trying to make contact, I would certainly do that. Of course I wouldn't foist it on him. Only if he imagined it would help him. Sure, what would it cost me?

T: I might cost you your sanity.

M: How so?

T: Believing a madman?

M: I don't see it. I'm free to believe whatever nonsense I like.

T: Will it not do you harm?

M: Not at all. If it's real it will do me good. If it's unreal it won't do me good. But it won't harm me.

T: Will it not harm the madman, if you believe his madness?

M: What would you have me do? Argue with him?

T: Would you carry the candle for him?

M: That's cute. It would depend on the degree of my compassion.

T: Oh, very good! You cannot predict that then?

M: Naturally I can not.

T: How about supernaturally?

M: I stay clear of that zoo.

T: Zoo?

M: Where people have locked themselves into cages until they turned into animals so that the gods outside won't harm them.

T: My my! That's very acute too. Did you think of that yourself or did you quote someone?

M: You're not a teacher if you have to ask that.

T: Remind me to discuss that with you when this session is over.

M: That sounds promising. Have you detected wisdom in me?

T: Does it matter to you whether I can tell or not?

M: I'd really prefer to be able to know it myself.

T: Well then. Know.

M: Knowledge is the growth of my body. When I know, I grow, because my body grows, Right away I want to communicate. I know that wisdom is within my grasp. I am the happiest man alive. You have done it. You have led me by the hand to the discovery of my wisdom. Is my joy the reward you would want?

T: No. My joy is in having met another wise human being. We are thin on the ground. Nevertheless there are enough of us to go around. Now that you know that you are capable of wisdom, how are you going to change your life?

M: I won't buy any lottery tickets, I can tell you that much.

T: That's funny. Why not?

M: Wisdom, so far as I can make out at the moment – in my most inward being, if I may say so – refuses to divide reality, such as into necessity and chance, into intention and accident, consciousness and unconsciousness – heaven and earth. Wisdom is proof of the connection. A wise man would never upset reality. He loves, above all, justice. He knows that reality is appropriate as it is and as it comes up, not to mention as it was. He believes that, even if it appears to him otherwise.

T: I would say: especially if it appears to him otherwise.

M: Wise cancels otherwise. I like that.

T: There were two men. Each had written a book. The first one had written for money. He guessed what people wanted and tried to produce it for them. The second one had had something to say. He tried to say it as clearly as possible. He had no idea what people wanted but he wisely imagined that since he was a human being among human beings on the earth and since all were connected, reality being whole, he would not have been given anything to say that was useless. So he went ahead in good faith and spoke out. I mean he wrote his book. But no one wanted to read it. This never bothered him. He simply wrote another one and offered it too and so on.

M: How long has this been going on then?

T: About thirty-five years.

M: And you're not concerned?

T: I realize that I can't know the time.

M: You'll continue to write, even though no one reads what you write?

T: Virtue, in the old sense of the word, is its own reward. I've decided that my work is limited to the writing of these books and to the careful preservation of them. I make no attempt to advertise. Why should I?

M: That attitude makes sense if you address people and they don't reply. But in the case of your books, how is anyone to know they're around to be read?

T: Oh I have informed acquaintances. I don't make a secret of it.

M: So you have no complaints?

T: None.

M: Why did you tell me about it?

T: Because I wanted you to know. You're an acquaintance now. Besides, you are to demonstrate, now that you have discovered your wisdom, what you can gain from it.

M: First I would much rather take several hours to contemplate that wisdom.

T: You mean – directly?

M: Yes, of course. Why not?

T: I'm amazed. You move fast. In one step you arrived where I did after travelling for miles.

M: Evidently you travelled those miles not only for yourself. But what, specifically, have you in mind?

T: That you should right away think of this wisdom as something to ponder.

M: I have to believe that if I ponder this wisdom I must make contact with the origin of it. I cannot imagine that I've always had it about me.

T: Why not? I say you have. You have had it since the cradle. But it was laid there. By the one who creates us. How should I know how you picture this!

M: I shall picture my father who has laid this wisdom into my cradle – into my human nature.

T: Splendid. Now what will you do with it?

M: I dare say I will know when the time comes.

T: Ah! You have no intention of applying it?

M: Come to think of it, this reminds me of your writing. I will lay this wisdom up like a treasure. It will give me rest. Eternal rest. Do you recall how I was when I arrived here? Like someone who needs a fix. Having discovered my wisdom I intend to ponder it, to lay up eternal rest – the way you lay up your books. Eventually the time will be ripe for action. An event will set the action off. That will then be perfect action. Spontaneous and totally responsible.

T: So what does it mean to be wise?

M: It means to respond to events with eternal rest from a storehouse that is filled when we apply our thought intelligently to the wisdom our father had laid into our human nature.

T: However did you arrive at such a conclusion so quickly!

M: You've arrived there before me. You straightened the path for me. Can I not tell how it all falls into place? I arrived here with nothing but my confessed foolishness and instead of rejecting me you suffered me gladly.

T: In a sense that was an act of gratitude.

M: How so?

T: The one who showed *me* where this wisdom lay buried in me had equally been there before me. I simply passed the favour on, as you no doubt will do some day. Now we have to go our separate ways for a while. When we meet again we will have much to talk about. It's such an immense pleasure to be wise!

*

10

Thinking Becomes Creation

"Out of the mouth of babes . . ." – I let the babe in myself talk and I listen very closely. Classical thinking applies itself, though we think we do it. It fools us a bit. At times it betrays us, outright; then we take the blame for that. We might have been otherwise. Those who take the blame for the devil conquer him.

Classical thinking divides and conquers. When there is nothing left to divide – and atoms cannot be divided, only split – creation wants to take over. Why in heaven's name would anyone be so misguided as not to comply! Creation is the goal of classical thinking. We divide and separate so as to get to the bottom of things. When we are there we can get started. Then the actual business of creation starts. Then we reach in and haul out, as much as we like, and there is no end to it. It pours out in abundance, great streams of life, four, or seven, or nine.

Classical means limited, means borders and fences, means definition towards fruition. Rational solutions are never final solutions, but in a direction, with a goal in view. Classical thinking is systematic and therefore it expects to find the stone which will not fit into the system. It cherishes that stone, because it knows that this stone, which on the surface looks no different from this and that, not comely, will eventually fit on the day of completion, on the lord's day, when the workers down tools, step outside and patiently/reverently await the crowning. "And he saw that I was good". That sight was the actual creativity at work. He saw, so that it would be good or, in a later version, "they waited for the kingdom to become visible". They downed tools and were glad, were gay, took no heed of the form that their particular completion, from outside, would take. If blood is involved, let's appreciate the colour of it.

Eventually, so we are led to believe, the workers cooperate eternally with the crowning agency. The notion of 'eternal' takes over once the classical division of 'internal/external' has succeeded. The kingdom is within/among you, so avoid the 'outer' darkness. Then it happens that those who have clung to the classical divisions, with their class-consciousness, get confused. Their brows wrinkle. For their sake we step 'back' for a moment onto the chessboard. They don't understand the mate position. How can they partake of the creative joy if they don't realize that chess is a game? This world was not to go on forever; we explain this to them. The system was preparatory. Chess is a friendly contest, not the living of life.

We sweep away all these pictorial animosities. The so-called world wars, the world in its death throes, then the cold war –

(who thinks of these names!) – not with a bang but a whimper. Or let's put it this way: first a couple of bangs, then a whimper.

Who can control creative levity! The stones themselves split. Songs pour out, roll like lava across the minds of men, women and children. Stars appear again in the heavens that are interconnected and founded on the new earth we discovered when we helped the gods heroically by parting the grass. Part the feathers and expose the succulent breast of the pigeon. Undo a few buttons, etc. ...

Who can unbutton the cosmos and expose human nature? They have looked for nature in every damned corner – into every Quark we bury our noses – until finally one gives up. Bugger the effort. We look for the wrong nature. We search in the outer darkness. Now please, just take your eyes off that chessboard for a moment. You have lost the game but found yourself. Let me explain. Metaphors, myths and mysteries, they're all here for our sake, like the Sabbath for man. Give yourself a shake, you look stunned. You only imagined that explosion. Splash some cold water on your face. Now don't get me wrong, when I say it's all in your mind, I don't trivialize; on the contrary, I recognize the tragedy of the situation. But let's at least recognize it. Trembling with fear is not the same as getting out of that house during the earthquake. The quake exists to get you out of the house, outdoors at last into the crystal sunshine. The bad weather is over for all time. But don't take my word for it. Get out there. I challenge you to be sane. It's all in your mind now and the incubation time is over. Let the birth-pangs not stiffen you. Repeated quick short breaths, that might help. It happens. It knows what it's doing. It's called human nature and your god is at home in it. Forget about nature now, about your natural history, your natural sciences, your para-natural, super-natural aerobics to impress the audience in your bones. Think human nature, not nature. Create!

*

33

Always again you dig in first to assure yourself of solid ground underfoot. The man who looks down on himself needs to look up to no one. You have this to overcome. Then you look up to the one who would never look down on you. He creates himself for you, like this and like that, out there, and you don't need to fear, I'll tell you why: because you have the redeeming vision. In your eye sits the god who maps out his world organically. The veil of the Maya, is that not another word simply for the human skin? What is that for you, your skin? Does it cover something? Is there an inside and an outside, a behind and an in front of? Is your skin not organic? Listen to your natural historian with his materialistic explanation; he will at least afford you that opportunity of a failure. In the new world, the skin of the Maya glows. Your beatific vision handles that very nicely, thank you. The secret is open. The mother is not to be neglected. The mother and the maiden, all rolled into one, overwhelming, these attributes of a virgin Mary. And what a relief, when Aphrodite has a few times pulled the wool over your eyes! That was to show you your failures. Woe betide those who insist that they shall have no failure. These are the classical drop-outs. They are blind and deaf and dumb precisely because they insist they have the only intelligence. For their sake we dig a large hole into the ground. Eventually they will need this protection. God is merciful, he supplies us with burial rites.

The new veil of the Maya, that allows us to eat one another's flesh so as to become one in the flesh too. But that lies so close at hand – so close to the bone – that it usually gets pushed into the remote distance. Well certainly, call it unusual. We are talking beauty here. The beauty of a man, of a woman, of a child. Is it always to destroy us? Is it always to terrify us, because we don't 'measure up'? If you don't measure up now, forget it. Adam and Eve in the garden sans fig leaf – that too was a look forward. Why would we call something lost if we didn't eventually expect to find it? That's only a very clever ruse, this classical division of the present into past and future; don't take it so seriously. You can't push your little boat out on history or prophesy. In the final analysis, they are not to hold water. But you are to push your little boat out. You are to leave your past behind so that it can turn up beside you as future. I hope this confuses you. You were far too certain, considering that you were certainly wrong. Clutching that chess board, your eyes riveted to those sixty-four squares – what, are you a housefly?

Your thought has only the one destination that suits it wonderfully and that is your true human nature. You fear that your human nature is not true? So don't fear. The truth is with you. Fear distorts things. Panic is a monster and it creates monsters. You don't scuttle it by bargaining. Instead know that the truth is with you. It's in you. Some years ago it plumbed your human nature. Now that it's navigable, push out your boat.

*

If only I knew how to make myself better understood! I'll make everything so clear that I understand it in my mind, before I say it or write it down. That's the classical response to the massive charge: "We can't understand you!" I know well enough, you lot out there, you want it set in darkness like aspic so that it fits into your unenlightened minds and stays there. I can guess what you mean by clarity. You are so used to prison fare that you want your bread caged. But for your sake I refuse to please you, and for my sake I refuse to comply with your wishes. The time has come, for me at least, to break out and breathe fresh air. First I will say what I have to say – and I do have something to say – and then we can get together on understanding it. Don't get me wrong, I know what I'm saying while I say it. The understanding of it is something else. 'Speak clearly!' That usually means: Tell me what I've heard before and what pleases me. It should mean: Let your thought and feeling stream out human-naturally. Be ready to pass from thinking to creation at a moment's notice and then create spontaneously, taking account of every available eventuality. There's no need to stop. What, were you arrested? You were probably speeding. The captain of that boat called creation has a nose for every breeze and for every doldrum. He knows what to do in a storm. For him there is never a scarcity of supply. Life is its own goal, eternally. Never look outside life, because there's no outside to it. It's all in your imagination or in your mind. What is? All these limitations, borders and fences! That's where they are and that's where they belong. Your mind is in fact measurement. Your reason and purpose for measuring? So that the stream will flow.

And yet strangely enough most of us measure so that the stream precisely won't flow. We fear that whatever comes out of us diminishes us, so we stop all the exits. Before we give time we ask: How long? Before we give life we ask: How much? By that time the opportunity has passed and we're left with the tail end of a bad taste in our mouth.

Let planning branch out into poetry; suddenly, in the twinkling of an eye. You should really count it all joy when your poetry is blocked and you have to return to planning, because that means that a new organ is being developed or that an old one has come to the end of its development. So don't collapse. Expand your capacity. Send a welcoming party out when you've heard that the king is on his way. And always behave as though he were just now on the way to you. Because he is. If he's not in your hand, he's in your elbow moving down to your hand.

Creativity can become almost entirely imitative. We behave like blanks on which the spirit is to leave his mark. Well, that's at least something. It's better than charging into the future and ignoring the present source of all fruitfulness. It's better than sleeping, than mere unconsciousness. But much better yet if we spur our horse on. We get lazy in the flesh, tardy in the mind, indigent in the body, tired in the soul and lethargic in the spirit. Instead of spirit we have lethargy, instead of soul – tiredness. You, you are the one to get your five horses into harness, to put them to work. We are here to create, not to complain, criticize and make lame excuses. Distinguish between yourself and your five horses.

*

Some get so far as to realize that "the traces of their days on earth / cannot in aeons be effaced" (Faust). Those are the fruits of our creation and those who make use of them have the advantage. But it takes an additional 'memory' for me to realize that I myself will never be effaced. That particular realization has to do with the rank of my creativity. Not *I* am mortal but only those parts of me that remain beyond my use, for whatever reason. Temporality affects me alright, but so that I have what it takes to create, to create such works as will point others in the same direction. Temporality is not my state, but a borrowed state, an adopted condition – for a time. Temporality pertains to me for the duration of my work. How was I initially transported outside or beyond this state of temporality, so that I am now free to condescend to it for the good of those who exist in it – and also of course for my own good, so as to be ever more confirmed in my eternal life? That's the one thing I refuse to touch on in these essays. Instead I take advantage of it and do demonstrably what I could not do if I had not been thus transported.

The winnings are for those who take them. For everyone like me there are a thousand who come to the end of their rational thought and then they turn back. Creativity just does not become them. They say that it's not in their nature and as we believe, so it is for us. All the arguments in the world to the contrary would only serve to fortify them in their position as rational animals. Then there are thousands who create but not with rank. They know that their thoughts are limited and limiting and this amounts to their integrity because it allows them, this knowledge, to step back and down before the great creative forces and energies that fill our universe, and in this 'resignation', as a philosopher has imagined it, they become carriers of potent, though obscure, messages from the gods to men, from the realm of law to the world in disorder. They transfer ideas from where they arise to where they become accessible. They are called messengers. Their thought may run deep but it never goes under. It may aim high but it never runs over. Ideas and laws, and the mighty forces and energies in existence, these are their masters and beyond them they know nothing. In them they take their refuge and in the absence of them they diminish.

However thought actually becomes creativity for those who know that their human nature is in truth immortal. They believe this and their belief has become knowledge. This change from believing, faith, to knowing, knowledge, is crucial to all their action and passion. It heralds the on-coming light that transforms the world and them along with it. They reveal this faith-knowledge to those who have eyes and ears to accept it. Down they dip with the world and men into water and fire, and up they come again, showing what it means to be cleansed for service and the truth. Their tolerance level is high because much that might grow makes its peace with sleep, with the fashions of culture and with next to no insight into human being specifically. Where they land they stay put, since any place for them is as good as another, guaranteed to offer abundance of material for care and concern, for understanding and love. They embrace their destiny, their fate, because they recognize it as their inheritance, as an immense treasure-house that has always been ready for them, and now, as they share out its contents, they themselves come finally into the joyful possession of them.

*

11

Time

Beginnings are extremely important. Not everyone can tell ahead of time how much time is available, so it's a good idea if we set our own clocks. We can always believe that the intelligence is equally present in the plan as in the execution.

If we believe that, then the petrol will always last to the end of the journey, not because we equate the destination with the catastrophe but because the one who fills the tank has access to the map.

Beginnings have quality. They define time itself. This in addition to their prediction of our selves as temporal. If we make the beginning, I mean that particular one, then we submit not only to time but to a species of time, a type or a sort of it. But that part of it has to surprise us. If, instead of walking, which would stand for the eternal rhythm in this comparison, we opt for transport, then this is like a beginning. That part of it is entirely up to us. We could have walked. But now that we chose transport we may keep our eyes open because we may end up on horseback, in an automobile or in an aircraft. The mode of transport – of time – is not open to our decision.

For those who never make a beginning, time does not exist. And since time does not exist for them, neither does eternity. This is both a bitter pill to swallow and a hard nut to crack. The body and the mind are involved. There is a problem to be solved and a sickness to be cured. Only in comparison to eternity, from the point of view of eternity, and therefore within the context of eternity – does time reveal to us its true character as a blessing, as a vehicle of happiness, of luck. Those who insist on remaining contained in time and curtailed by time – and we cannot help but conclude that they insist, since eternity is equally open to all – are called historic beings, by themselves. They call one another historic beings because they believe that eternity is beyond them and that periods of time must describe something they call human life. We would say that only one variety of time is available to them, but this would be as incorrect as it must seem misleading, since they are curtailed by time and contained in it. They assume, for example, that they can control and master time. Again and again they make this assumption, in spite of what must seem to outsiders to be frequent sobering experiences. They are like people on a train in a totally unfamiliar country who try forever to predict the event of the next stop from the pattern of all previous stops. With each stop the past pattern changes and the next prediction is undertaken with renewed hope. At times, entirely by accident, a prediction falls out accurate, whereupon the pattern that gave rise to it is adopted as the norm for all future predictions – but then a new generation is born and the next stop is very late, or very early –reasons for this are then deduced from the description of the stop.

Those who make a beginning stand suspended with one leg in eternity and one in time and they know that they stand firm. They are not in the predicament of the one who has one foot on dry land and one in the boat and then the boat begins to move. They themselves make the beginning, not time. For that reason time is swathed in beauty. Everything moves in relation to everything else and everything is related to everything else. There are a million names and as many numbers. A waterfall cascades over the lip of a cliff. Metaphysics is afoot. A roebuck at the edge of the forest contemplates the bedewed meadow. Coordinate systems tumble out of the sky, break open and reveal institutions for mankind. A stratospheric breath sweeps across the beach, moans in the pine forest, piles wave upon wave against storehouses called rock. Symbol, legend – the principle of dynastic rule – these have a field day. One would swear by these changes, except for that one leg in eternity; except for the solid foundation and the house which is home.

So every beginning is an excursion from home into time, and into some kind of time. All these types, sorts, kinds and varieties of time one simply calls time – once back home. Meanwhile time has taken on a splendour or become magnificent. It dances or sings or disports itself as a poem. Perhaps it organizes the crystal of an experience by reflecting upon itself and commenting to the flowers in the field. Then philosophy takes a turn, called the love of knowledge and culminating in the knowledge of love.

After every beginning comes the middle when deception tempts. The day is high but we say that we die. A millennium passes out but we say that panic enters. Fullness is taken for scarcity, joy for misery, the son of man for the great pretender. Middles have to be like this, so that the men are separated from the boys and so that the boys can return to the gymnasium and the men carry on to bigger and better things. Often, in the middle, a little black man waves a sign on which characters depict the running out of time. Boys collapse by the side of the road, lungs full of dust. Men drink and push past the little demon who was cut out of cardboard and invisible in any case. The boys can make another beginning, another time. The sun on the backs of their elders and the dust from their feet sometimes blind and suffocate, but there must be a testing. A temptation to the feeble becomes a test for the strong.

Another idle – or noon-phenomenon is the mental picture as justification. Justification for what? Why, for never having begun. Best of all is not to have been born. The Shropshire lad pulls his cap over his eyes because the wood's in trouble. Homer lives on via Troy and Rome but is refused access to the market place on account of an unsigned visa. Morality in the teeth of lemmings is carried into the sea. In short, one believes one's own rubbish rather than creation and invariably succumbs to a stomach ache. One is sorry one started.

But all these philandering flights of sluggishness can be handed over, to that master of all non-starters called death. Then his broom sweeps the threshing floor clean. He loves to serve others, does death, if others see through him. He died once but then was reborn, as the servant of potential gods. Not that he has the slightest notion as to the nature of the time, but he knows what time it is, beginning, middle or end, and in that capacity, a princely one for my money, he becomes indispensible. He searches in my eyes now. A nod is as good as a wink to him. Nothing demonstrative, he desires to be kept in his place, though at times he makes work for the boys. At times he sits out on the veranda in a rocker, a pipe in his mouth, the crows massing around the factory chimney, and from the sheer sweet appearance of him you would not for one moment believe he was hollow, worm-infested, loaded down by worries about mortgages, by scruples concerning paranormal experiences, by the inability to find an end.

*

12

The Force Against Which Nothing Can Stand

That there is a force that breaks through all hindrances – but no one would believe that unless it were demonstrated. So it occurs to the demonstrator that these hindrances should be classified – but nothing of the sort. Experience – and the desire to praise – brings them on, soon enough and in the right order.

If you set yourself a task, you have no idea ahead of time how the challenges will crop up. Every real advance is also an overcoming, so that you can make up your mind, ahead of time. Every date and every locality produces its own enemies to progress – so that progress shall be lively and strong.

*

The sickening realization that things are going wrong and you don't know how to cope. Of course they are going wrong in comparison to what you are calling right. The way you pictured it to yourself, that was right. Now the course of events does not match your picture. You decided that by doing X you would bring Y about. Instead M happened. So you scuttle your picture. What you did is done, forget about it. Return to the purity of your heart. Problems that pretend to be links in a chain that binds days, weeks, months together need to be particularized. This amounts to an identification with the present day. 'What?' you protest. 'Am I to keep this up for the unforeseeable future?' – Today stops tonight. Tomorrow anything could happen, literally.

A heartfelt concentration. A limitation, by yourself, of yourself, to what is your own business. That means leaving your hands off a great deal. It also means emphasis on a particular thing. And that particular thing must be the force that overcomes all hindrances. I have it in mind, so I suppose that this is not a true essay. On the other hand I would always have it in mind, no matter what I do. But an essay should not be *about* anything, not even about the force that overcomes all hindrances – that thrives on hindrances. So this is the last I'll mention of it.

*

The popular ambitions ring me round. This person I have in mind, she does good work for money. So why don't I stay out of her way! She does it for me too, her good work, if I pay her the money, but suddenly she asks: 'Would you do this to please me? But only if you want.' – It's a come-on and a disclaimer, rolled into one. On analysis, she was perfectly in her rights. Her idea is, to get as much as she can for money. That mentality usually bamboozles me, though it makes perfectly good sense. The children of Mammon are incomparable. They were christianized to a much greater extent at one time, so I believe, but wherever the Christianity has peeled off, there we have cold, calculating finance. You might as well blame a bird for flying once its clipped wing-feathers have grown back. I really do believe that Christianity clipped their wings. It made them feel bad for being children of Mammon. They became ashamed of their parentage. For centuries they pretended to this hypothetical religion and it cramped their style. It put them under a most

43

unusual pressure. And the most uncommon energies were released due to his pressure. I think of the extinct arts and sciences, of imperialism dating back to the crusades and beyond. Mighty cathedrals, vast explorations – well, somebody had to do it. Why not put the children of Mammon under this hypocritical pressure and then they'll do the right thing for the wrong reason and all for a slap on the back and a mention in the great history book. You still hear idiotic echoes today: 'Let (country of your choice) be a leader among nations again!!) I mean, I ask you – when you see youngsters playing cowboys and Indians and fighting over who gets to be the chief, you smile. But these are grown people, and because they've been turned – or turned themselves, it's all the same – into representatives of the popular ambition, we listen to them and don't smile. Still today? So what has changed? Has the clock run down? Every day since the resurrection of Jesus is the day of the lord for those who have bought the right calendar. The rest is paraphernalia; parerga and paralipomena. The rest is amusement for the lads on holiday. I cannot for the life of me take it seriously, though god knows I try at times and go through my little phases, as with her who asked me to fall in with her plans and I stupidly took her up on her suggestion. There's no reason at all for filling you in, Theophilus, on any of the particulars. The bur is stuck in my fur and it irritates me, and I know it's my own fault, for scrambling through the underbrush.

*

A change of topic. We arrange a few thoughts. We know that these are thoughts of our own that have half happened to us and half been pictured by us. We associate certain schemata with them. These are like ghosts. Some people call this imagination but it ain't. What it is, rather than imagination, is a fearful projection of darkness, of shadow, so that we can make out the thought that has happened to us. I'm mixing up here what can be done, what is usually done and what we ought to do.

44

What we call our thoughts – not our thought – are in fact fearful projections. We can accept that this is so and take it from there or we can try to explain why anyone would fear – what? Obviously we fear what we suppose comes too close to us. Do we give a name to whatever stimulates not our thoughts but our thought? Do we say that something is *given* to us, by someone? Or do we satisfy ourselves by saying that suddenly something, or someone, is here which, or who, was not here?

All this depends on date and place, on culture and tradition. What counts is what we do at that moment in time, and our comprehension of what it was that led to that moment of – inspiration? – should entirely serve what we do. In a very important sense our notion of the past, even of such a thing as a past, should always be made to serve, by ourselves, our present action. We should realize that we invent a past in the first place to help us with the present day. We should never tire of reminding one another of that. If I'm convinced that it would help us now to think of Henry VIII of England as a tiger in drag then I should have a go at that particular presentation. I would be doing it intentionally, aware of what I was doing, not fearfully, as an accidental projection – which I would then feel panic-bound to defend to the hilt.

How much, in the world, at an given time, is not built on fearful projections – on thoughts!

Quite a different thing from a fearful, accidental projection is a thoughtful presentation. One woman hears she's pregnant and says: "Damn it! And I was so careful too!" Then she runs to the abortionist. The other one says something like: "I'm the handmaid of the Lord. Let His will be done." What we have is the difference between a fearful projection and an honourable presentation.

Thoughts are the darkness we project against new light, so that we end up with seemingly manipulable ghosts. Test it, give it something to eat. Make your thoughts matter. Try it. It won't work. Thoughts can never be made to matter. They can be built up into huge systems, world-duplicates, and they keep the new light back, at a distance, for a short time. Then they crumble.

But thought can be made to matter. That's how I started this topic. If you have projected a few thoughts, accidentally, while you weren't looking (the son of man has to come when we're not looking) then take your time now and submit them to thought, subject them to thought, in short – decimate them. No one can come to the Messiah who hasn't hated his brother. It doesn't have to be a huge hate and it mustn't go on once you've noticed it. Then you intentionally love your brother and decimate that hate. It's called loving your enemy, and it turns everything around. Your brother, who was your enemy while you hated him, becomes your friend. The word of god, which you accidentally feared, becomes your flesh. Submitting those fearful thought projections, those ghosts, to your creative thought, this decimates those ghosts and the light you obscured in your initial panic enlightens you properly now. The few thoughts that you arranged are dissolved by your thought. I'm assuming that you know how to think, how to love; that you know how to love your enemy, how to think your thoughts.

Thinking your thoughts is like loving your enemy? No, it's not at all like that. It is that. Your thoughts are your enemies. To think a thought is to confront a ghost with the true reality of good spirit. Manipulating thoughts, multiplying them, painting them pink and purple, that's not thinking. Appeasing your enemy, tolerating him, telling him a pack of lies to keep him off your back, that's not love; it's the cowardice of a scoundrel.

But don't be in despair because once again you find yourself with thoughts. As you get better at thinking, at intentional, creative thinking, such as when you make a thoughtful beginning (see previous essay) so you will notice fewer, small thoughts sooner, and you will think these with greater consequence and expedition. The life you find is not the life you keep. The thoughts you find yourself with are not the ones that matter. The thought you live, the thought you present – matters. So you have to overcome your thoughts. For that you need the force that can overcome anything. Your thoughts are the most difficult things to overcome – along with your feelings, your emotions, your moods and sentiments, etc.

The force against which nothing can stand – is not a force at all, really, but simple human natural affection.

Have I let the cat out of the bag? Not really. Anything can and will be misunderstood, let's not kid ourselves. Those who see come to the light and those who don't see get used to the darkness. All we can do is make reality tangible for those who have fingertips. Or perhaps we can do just a little more. We can write essays, for example, where we make ourselves so scarce that the reader is nearly obliged to agree that he has what it takes to make his life matter.

* * *

13

The Truth

The truth. The cold, unveiled truth. And perhaps no embarrassment, no sense of shame, above all not that hollow feeling that comes along, when it has all been said – the whole truth.

Tell me the truth, she says, pointing to his psyche, as if she were indicating a maelstrom and demanding therein a sound foothold. The truth? Quickly he would have to cobble something together, to satisfy the tigress in her. Why is the will to truth such a predator?

The enigmatic aspect of the will to truth is calculated to create a smoke-screen for foreign judgment. How can anyone demand that I should be truthful? And to do it at a certain time! I would have to prepare myself for a couple of months. A breakdown of the nerves would prove useful. The customary household of the nerves is after all founded on a steady, reliable income of perfectionism. Things must be just so. Otherwise – no temper. So truth here means confinement to perfection.

Truth can also mean 'the ring of beauty'. This is truth imagined on holiday in the Bahamas. The face of it pleases. The casual remark can set it off. In league with the moon, in search of a galaxy, it seduces. Artists sharpen their pencils here and steal a glance at the competition. 'Well-functioning', 'just' – words to describe examples of it. Also 'the magic moment'. It can enter via some sense and travel the gamut of emotion from self-sacrifice to a correct appreciation of the absurd. The woods at night are fraught with dreams of it.

Then the historic truth: – which is why he calls her 'his precious' at ten fifteen and at ten twenty five he attacks her, leads her astray, abuses her trust in him. What has happened during those ten minutes? Presumably the truth has changed. Or she has. Or he has. Possibly they both, or all three have. The maelstrom again. What he meant after all was not intended for eternity. Shouldn't she have known that? According to her, he really should have told her. He should have said: 'The truth, my dear, adheres to moments. What is true now is not necessarily true now, because a second has passed. If you have allowed yourself to be misled to build altars to the truth and fly standards over them, that is your affair. You cannot expect reality to function in line with your notion of fair-mindedness. A sense of honour is all very well but when a rage builds up or a mood take its toll, the mask of truth comes down, while behind it – but I would not trouble you. Have you not managed ever so well so far! Your popularity shall remain inviolate, only arm yourself with the appropriate medication.

The gallant truth comes next, which is as we would like it. Tell me where the shoe pinches and let me buy you a new pair of shoes. The trick is never to be friendless. A true and gallant friend will tell you what you want to hear. You may not know what to do with it afterwards but then you can shake yourself free of it, as of a joke. Meanwhile the crisis has passed. Joy reigns supreme again. So let's not assume, Doctor Freud, that the truth may be approached in terms of angel worship. The angels themselves cannot behave as they wish in the absence of the truth, because they have their orders and end up dumbfounded if you get on your knees in front of their pictures. Hence that cataract of ideas every now and again when a culture is forced to correct itself after a decade, or a century, of blatant bloody-mindedness hand in hand with extolled values. Gallantry serves an unknown master and although it may flinch in the cold, it never runs away from it because even the elements are acknowledged by it as moral. At the same time discipline is larger than this life. Which means you have to lie for the truth. You respect illusions and you let sleeping dogs lie, at most hoping to influence their dreams. The truth of the moment is never challenged by the gallant truth and should a kangaroo sprout wings or compose music. God is all-powerful, nothing is impossible for god. If a stone falls when it is pushed over the edge, then that might well be surprising, though it has happened before. If a young man looks into himself and discovers there the unknown, for the umpteenth time, that is no reason to presume that he should not now quickly join the circus. Many have joined the circus and travelled on enlightened. Whatever it is that challenges our faculties, we have the god-given choice to call it hellish or holy.

*

The very compartmentalization of the truth into truths can be – well – truthful. Or not. It depends on who does it. Because, my friend, take this on board now if you can manage it and still keep your coracle upright: as you divide the truth so you divide your self. Some have a mission for dividing their self. They have no self to start with, and then they absorb, for the occasion of a work, the prevalent self of the times, from their im-

49

mediate vicinity. And this they divide then. They practice a critique on the self they foster for the time being. Their attitude towards this self is itself crucial of course. Not every artist is familiar with the 'son of man'. The process of adoption can go far, however. The aristocrat of the word says straight out: 'This is I,' and deals with the consequences. However only the aristocrat has the knowledge that if he dies for others he lives again. Your popular artist is quite right to fear death and deprivation because for him it's an accident if he should recoup. He has no guarantee. If he does pick up again, after weight-loss, he counts himself lucky. He might even get into the habit of gambling for high stakes.

This is to look away entirely from those tragic cases that mistake something for their own self – which they must preserve, model and exhibit.

Let's ask in any case, is there any such thing as a self that is not an absorbed race consciousness – the self-consciousness of the race, the corporate image, the mass psyche – accidentally internalized? Look at it this way: You are infected as by the bacillus, the virus, of the collective consciousness and you have the choice: Do you understand this and do you then make something of this 'donum' or do you not even catch on but you stumble through life forever infected to death. And if recognition does happen to you, how far do you take it? To the bitter end where it turns into sweetness, or a quarter of the way, where you feel yourself superior because you detect a sham but you set no example; or halfway, where you meander between success and failure, between self-importance and self-mutilation – or three-quarters, addicted to heroic feats of greatness and seductive towards martyrdom.

Is there a self that doesn't begin – isn't transferred – as a 'bug'? 'What's wrong with you, you look sick?' 'I've caught a bug.' 'Ah, that explains everything.'

However, let's also be honourable and remind one another that we cannot have the slightest true notion of the race, of mankind, of society and community, if we don't say yes to the infection and turn it into affection.

So suddenly I am landed back with my self, but this time it's mine because I do something with it, because I 'raise the son of man'. It's not mine by accident, like my sickness, but by birthright and investment. That's a different sort of ownership altogether. Call it genitive. It's mine because I generate growth with it. Some moneymen understand that very well, about their own particular god. The money market speculator would never sit down to count his pennies, he'd be too busy with investments. In the same way the Messiah is hardly surprised that baskets of crumbs are left over. Eventually he divides up himself, as the truth, and there's always a surfeit.

*

So it nearly comes down to the truth being one another's burden which we carry gladly.

At the moment I find that easy to say because I can barely drag myself around. This essay has cost me more than I care to admit. But I intend to finish it. It has finished me, the least I can do now is finish *it*.

Which brings me to the point of the new truth. It doesn't fit into any category because we haven't laid a finger on it yet. I'm completely divided and I wait. The new truth is my hope. I remain open to it, though I'd like nothing better than to go permanently asleep now. My flesh hangs on me like dead weight. But then I begin to yawn. Such yawning as nearly blinds me for four seconds. And then I heave sighs such as have never been heard. Black sighs, closely akin to moans. And more yawning. The renewal is taking place. Happily no one is near me now, on the popular front; it would take a human being to understand what's going on, and to bear with me. If my wife were here, she would do it, because she is also my friend and companion.

The perfection of new truth naturally forces us into a corner first. That's not entirely true. We feel forced into a corner. Anyway, I do. The reason for that doesn't lie in the truth, however, but in me. My last little bit of self I cannot divide by dividing the truth but it has to be removed. I describe at the moment what it's like to have my last little bit of self removed by the new truth. I don't for one moment assume that anyone could find this essay pleasant to read. But the truth is not pleasant. It clashes with our self. It contradicts the popular unconsciousness. It challenges the tradition of the people. And my last little bit of self is popular, is mankind-related, not related to you. So, since my ambition is to communicate with you, not with mankind or the people, I have to divide the truth – i.e. my self – until none of it is left, so that the new truth can appear on the horizon – or on the clouds. Then we finally have our common human denominator. Then we can agree and say: Yes, the truth matters to us. We would rather speak the truth than anything else. We look forward to being renewed by the truth and we are ever so thankful that when we have divided the truth as far and as much as we can, there is still new truth, our reward, in its own good time, which can never be caused by us as if it were a mechanical thing. The new truth is personal – and therefore honourable. I might as well dictate to you what you 'should', what you should be, as to the truth; it wouldn't work. All I can do is cheerfully depend on it, even if I feel that I've somehow been walked into the mud under my feet. And if I trust and insist that the truth will see me through, then he won't let me down. Sure, haven't I made a way of life of that? Is my life not based on that presupposition? Haven't I taken pains to make any other presupposition extremely awkward for myself?

Of course I've had help. Even at the beginning, when I was full of my self, I was lured by the truth, haunted by it, and nothing else would do for me, but I had to have him as my result, as my reward, so that any other result became doubtful, any other reward false. Now I think I may nearly have the strength to cope with the reaction to an essay such as this. Or let's say: With the total lack of response.

* * *

14

<h2 style="text-align:center">The Incarnate Spirit</h2>

There is such a longing in spirit itself, as we experience it in our innermost fibre, to unite itself with flesh, that most of our illnesses, at least the more mental ones, can be explained out of a certain indifference we maintain in the light of that longing. If the smallest portion of spirit allotted to us is forced, by our ignorance and hard-heartedness, to bypass the destination it seeks, namely our flesh, then this is not simply a loss for us, but for all those who, in our vicinity, have, after all, a communal right to co-benefit. There is more to it than that. If the spirit touches us – and by the spirit I mean good spirit – but we fail to respond, perhaps not only in our freedom to do so but even in our duty as ordinary human beings, then quite honestly we have placed ourselves in line for a setback or two. We cannot, once stirred by the spirit and not having responded, return unscathed and with impunity, to how we were and who we were prior to that stirring. As for any attendant unpleasantness, we have of course brought it on ourselves and need not pretend that some agent exists who has it in for us or who, upon fair judgment, raps our knuckles.

A response to the spirit's stirring, to the spirit's imitation, if you prefer – and initially it's the most polite invitation imaginable – such a response, by ourselves, is not to be conceived of, within this present context of inquiry, as other than perfectly and utterly natural. A favourite metaphor here translates nature as the bride and the spirit as the bridegroom. The bride's re-

53

sponse is a natural one. She is not given to deceitful assent or coy denial, but she does perhaps make some small effort to rid herself of any vestige of such tendencies, before she speaks as she thinks and feels, precisely at that moment. She responds truly, and naturally. If she gives herself, she does so as she is, not as she pretends to be or as she would prefer to be seen. We assume, of course, that she is someone, someone unique and particular, not a mere myth. A natural response presupposes a singular being and not one from the crowd. And when she does give herself, lo and behold, it's not a sacrifice, not an annihilation of self in another self, not a submergence of her intelligent personality in a marital state, but she becomes even more who she is, due to the union, assuming she has entered into it with her own eyes open and of her own free will. She becomes even more who she was, let's put it that way.

We can contemplate the metaphor imaginatively and draw a lesson or two. We can also find ourselves predisposed, by our inward acceptance of it, to a course of more practical understanding. In that case we cannot avoid coming to terms with what we mean by our own human nature. If we are to be capable of a truly natural response to good spirit, there must be within us some capacity, some power, that we were born with, naturally, and that is either true or at least lends itself willingly to the truth. If we believe that exists in us, we're off with a flourish. But if we have our doubts, our misgivings, our scruples, then there is one thing and one thing only for us to do, immediately, and that is the most expedient removal of those scruples and doubts. However we go about this removal, forthrightly or diffidently, thoroughly or piecemeal, that is how our responsive human nature will reveal itself to us. Always and again, as we live and work, there is this correspondence between how we go about the overcoming of inhibitions to our true human nature and how we are able to be naturally. A desire for truth and a will to truth is both indispensible to the efforts we undertake and guaranteed to our actual response. Truth runs like a common denominator through the preparation and the act of acceptance alike. This is the case whether we are born, endowed naturally, with a modicum of truth or else lend our nature to the truth, as revealed to us and as discovered by ourselves. The one who is the truth exists on both sides of the cradle and grave.

*

Given now that we believe in such a thing as a natural response to the good spirit, or to good spirit, we have to guard against a tragically common error that besets the modern appeal to spirit. This error is so ingrained in us, due both to cultural sanction and individual predisposition, that we lean on it repeatedly without knowing that we do – and so we topple. We tend to lean on it even – and therein of course lies the tragedy – while we analyse with the best of wills the various and manifold failures and half-successes of our appeals to spirit. Simply described, and at the risk of obscurity, the error is an attempt at the realization of disembodied spirit. It's like trying to enjoy the festivities and the meal by standing outside the hall and looking in through the window. Those who participate inside undoubtedly have the advantage. So that we don't slide off on the side of the parable, let's right away describe the error from the other side, specifically, as an ignorance of the way of all flesh as endowed with spirit.

It would do for us to have the right way of it on at least one side, but it helps if we can get at this problem with both hands, from both sides. We see, then, that there is something wrong, or at least not quite appropriate, in our attempt to 'realize spirit', because in an important sense the good spirit we mean is already real, so that the thing that remains for us to do can not be called straight out a realization of it. Presumption lies that way, and ultimate disaster. So before we do anything at all we need, so it seems, to be informed of the fundamental fact that the spirit to which our response is, by that very spirit, solicited, and to which we, as natural human beings, should wish to respond and in isolated cases even tend to respond – that this spirit is no less human than divine and no less divine than human. I formulate what I mean in this manner advisedly. The spirit we have to do with lends itself to appropriation as human, which is handy, you have to admit, and at the same time we may appeal to it as godly, or divine, which suits us no end at times. A quick comparison hopefully won't short-circuit our perception: there is the penny itself, and then we have, depending on how we hold it, the reverse or the obverse side; there is the Messiah, or the Christ, and then we have, depending on our approach, the human or the divine aspect of spirit. The Messiah is not a spirit, first of all, just as a penny is not a turn of one side or the other. This in itself is of crucial importance. Then, the penny is not one side or the other, just a the spirit that proceeds from the Messiah is not 'merely' human or 'purely' divine, as we sometimes like to put it in our befuddled minds, but either and both (in the absence of the 'merely' and 'purely').

*

Assuming now that we have a more correct appreciation of what is meant by the spirit available to us and desirous of our response, we can turn to a more just appraisal of what it is we ourselves may or must come up with (freely or dutifully) in order to avail ourselves of all the benefits so generously extended to us by the Messiah as his spirit.

First of all, it makes sense that our response should be natural, because it is spirit we respond to, and then it should seem obvious that our response must be human, not angelic, animal or demonic, since we are, presumably, human beings, not angels, animals or demons. Neither, of course, can we vegetate our way into the good graces of spirit.

Keeping in mind the human-natural factor, we may next add the element of work into our consideration of what is required. We don't take spirit into ourselves like bottles take in water,

56

remaining themselves unchanged, but we receive it by giving it, like anything that has to do with life. The work we do may amount to both preparation and execution, it may even be mostly one or the other, but as work it's essential, if we are to get anywhere and not merely to stand still until we fall back.

Thirdly there is the ethical element. What we do, our works, must somehow be available and accessible to others. It won't do if we propose we might develop or even grow privately in ourselves, or publicly, as egos. Our works must be rooted organically in ourselves, which argues against publicity, while at the same time other human beings have the benefit of them if they wish to avail themselves, either by observing our exemplary behaviour, or by taking advantage of our serviceable deeds, or even by knowing us through our creative works, and this argues against privacy of any sort, against exclusiveness, dogma, club membership and that sort of thing.

The work we do truly in response to the spirit is therefore always done to some extent, and eventually first and foremost – for others. And how do I bridge the existential gap between me and you? By loving you. My works must not only be human-natural (rather than spectral or mechanical) but also motivated by love, and specifically by my love of you, whether I like you or not, and especially if I dislike or even hate you.

In the light of day, not privately or publicly, do I want to do my work, while the energy I consume and the bridge that allows me to arrive where you are is live, and even human-natural affection.

Eventually I am inspired in my work, so that the spirit to which I have managed to respond actually now supports and strengthens me, in greater works, and then it teaches me, intuitively, because I have shown how I am open to the needs and shortcomings of others, in a spirit of forgiveness, of magnanimity, and greatest of all, of mercy. Eventually all this may transpire, if I keep my nose clean and to the grindstone. But

57

first of all I have to make that human natural and personal working response. And in that initial response, when we initiate an engagement with the spirit that has moved us, is involved what we call our flesh. This is the elemental aspect of our commitment, and it won't do to pretend that the carnal is negligible or absent, or perhaps even to be denigrated and cut off or sacrificed. Our flesh is not unholy. Our flesh is to be lifted up by the messianic spirit and to be united to itself, so that even carnally we are one with the one who loves us and whom we love.

Especially those who are touched by good spirit and not aware of what that means are in need of our working love and of our loving work, since they represent to people and the world all that is outcast and rejected. So are we to cast them out and to reject them? If we accept them and include them in our midst, not we as philosophers, as Buddhists or as Socialists but we as individual and communal human beings, then we demonstrate most strikingly and successfully to the world and to people, how the spirit that is good fulfils and completes. But more than that, we actually create for ourselves the elementary and fundamental preconditions for our own completion and fulfilment – because this spirit that is good can satisfy its desire in us by becoming, in us, flesh; incarnate.

Is it strange and wonderful that spirit should desire to become flesh, in particular human flesh? Until we are cleansed and chastened and until we have initiated a working response to this loving spirit, are we not veritably possessed in the flesh by hateful, bad and evil spirit? Are we not physically incapacitated, even crippled by it, rendered semi-conscious, sleepy and unaware of it, so that we become, at best, indifferent to one another and at worst invidious? Our lukewarm and suspicious attitudes, what are they but bad spirit incarnate?

So it lies in the nature of spirit to become inspired nature, if I may put it that way, and we ourselves as human beings have no greater or more noble task than to rid ourselves of bad and false and pretentious spirit and to invite into our flesh good spirit, and even the good spirit.

It's all good news. Where we are hypocrites – good news, there we have capacity for being instead friends of the truth and of one another in truth. Where we are cowards – good news, there we have the fibre for courage to stand up against the fear we inspire in another. Two realizations are needful. One, that we or others are enthralled by evil, captivated by wickedness. Two, that the good spirit is desirous to free us from those fetters and to unite us to itself in a union that is best described as eternal life.

*

Incarnate spirit is finally real, so we need to look no further. But until then we need to look – and to do. Study is not enough, there must be action, and action of a specific order. Due to our charitable exertion we are open and receptive to good spirit. By way of our loving sufferance of one another we actually respond to the spirit that invites us, and we should not be surprised that the invitation at first seems to be shrouded in pain and discomfort and inconvenience, since we became attached to nonsense incarnate and now we are being nudged against the grain. Our modern and sickening confusion is a sign that good spirit seeks us in the flesh.

* * * * *